W9-BAT-405

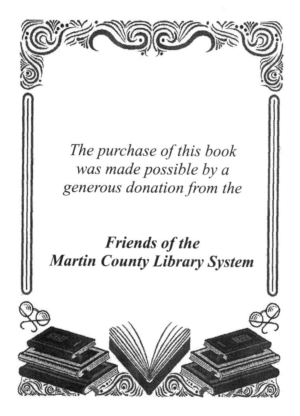

GLOWING with ELECTRICITY

Science Adventures with Glenda the Origami Firefly

by Thomas Kingsley Troupe

illustrated by Jamey Christoph

PICTURE WINDOW BOOKS
a capstone imprint

As the sun set in the countryside, a girl
finished the last fold of her origami firefly.
She held it up and smiled.

"I'll call you Glenda," she whispered.
She quickly attached Glenda to a mobile
that hung from the porch.

Glenda danced in the breeze with the other paper
shapes. Soon a real firefly flew up to meet her.

"Hi," the real firefly said.
"I'm MOLLY."

"Hi, I'm GLenda.
HOW are you?"

"NOt SO good. We fireflies wanted to
have a party. But we can't see ourselves
gLOW with that bright thing shining like
that. Can you help us?"

"Oh? That's a light. If you turn off the electricity, the light will go off."

"Electricity?" asked Molly. "What's that?"

"Please unhook me from this string, and I'll explain," Glenda said.

5

"Electricity gives power to things. That light, the TV inside the house, even that lawn mower—all of them use electricity to work."

"Okay. But where does electricity come from?"

"That's the best part. Electricity starts at the smallest of places—within an atom. Atoms make up everything you see."

"Really?" Molly looked around. "Everything?"

"They're too tiny to see," Glenda said. "But part of these tiny atoms are even tinier things called electrons."

"So imagine the center of an atom as a ball called a **nucleus.** Inside the nucleus are small blue balls and small red balls. The blue balls are **protons,** and the red balls are **neutrons.**"

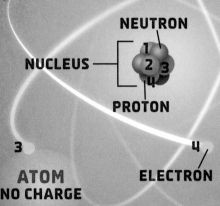

NEUTRON

NUCLEUS

PROTON

ATOM
NO CHARGE

ELECTRON

"Ok, but What about the **electrons?**"

"Well, a bunch of green balls called **electrons** are flying around the nucleus. If there's an **equal number** of electrons and protons in an atom, there's **no electrical charge.**"

"What if there's an **unequal** number?" Molly asked.

"If there are more electrons in an atom, the atom has an overall **negative charge**."

ATOM
NEGATIVE
CHARGE

"And if there are more protons?" Molly asked. "The atom has an overall **positive charge**?"

"**Right,**" Glenda said. "And when these charges move, **electricity** is formed."

ATOM
POSITIVE
CHARGE

STATIC ELECTRICITY

Ever rubbed a balloon on your hair? When you do that, you're moving electrons from your hair to the balloon. Static electricity is created, making your hair stand on end, or causing the balloon to cling to you. When these charges move all at once, you might feel a shock.

"Here's where things get interesting. A few electrons moving aren't enough to power a light."

"Really? How many are needed?"

"A lot. And the place where that happens is a power plant. It's a big building with machines called generators."

"A generator? This sounds tricky."

"It's not too tricky," Glenda said. "Most generators have a magnet that spins past a loop of metal wire. This movement keeps the electrons flowing."

"And that makes lots of electricity?" Molly asked.

"Yes," Glenda said. "And there are power plants all over the world!"

The fireflies flew near the small creek running along the farm.

"Some power plants rely on nature to keep them running."

"HOW SO?" Molly asked.

"Some power plants use the power of falling water, like this creek, but much bigger. The water falls into the plant, spinning a propeller-shaped turbine. The turbine turns the magnets inside the generator, creating electricity."

"Water power!"

"The sun is also a great source of power," Glenda said. "Solar panels can take heat and light energy from the sun and store it in batteries. The batteries can then be used to make electricity."

"Nature is awesome," Molly said.

As if water and sunlight weren't enough, generators can also be powered by wind. Those giant windmills out in the country aren't just cool to look at. They spin, and in turn spin the generator below, creating electricity.

SOLAR PANELS

"We've still got the problem with the light. No one will see your friends glow with it still on."

Molly sighed. "Yes," she said. "But I'm still wondering HOW all that electricity gets around."

"See those black wires connected to the house?"

"I thought they were just really thick spiderwebs."

"They're called **power lines**," said Glenda. "Electricity travels through the lines from the power plant to homes. It also travels to businesses and any other places that need power."

TRANSFORMERS

"Then what are those big silver things?" asked Molly.

"They're **transformers**," Glenda said. "When electricity comes from the power plant, it's really strong. A transformer takes the electricity and makes it weaker, so it's safer to use in houses."

Electricity passes through many different transformers along its journey. Some transformers knock the voltage, or strength of the current, down. Others can raise the voltage. If a house received a power plant's full voltage, it would be very dangerous to humans!

"I wish there was a way to turn off the light, so we could have our firefly party."

"All we have to do is block the electricity circuit."

"Huh? What's a circuit?"

"Electricity needs to follow a path, or a circuit. It's like a loop. Inside the house electricity travels through wires in the walls. If you block the path, the electricity is cut off."

"So how do we do that?"

"Call your friends over. I have an idea!"

"We turn off the
light switch!"

"How does it work?"

"Right now it's on. That means
the circuit is complete. When we
turn off the switch, the flow of
electricity will be blocked. When
the circuit is blocked—"

"The light goes off!"
Molly finished.

The fireflies all flew up to the switch. One sat on the switch, then another, and another. The fireflies were piled on top of one another.

Finally, the switch went down!

"Thanks for all of your help!" Molly said. "Now we can have our party!"

"You're welcome," Glenda said. "I suppose you should put me back up on my string."

"Why would I do that?" asked Molly. "Aren't you coming to the party?"

"I don't know. What's the party for?"

"Why, the party is for you, Glenda! Welcome to the firefly club!"

From that night on, Glenda felt like a real firefly. In fact, she was so happy, her smile made her glow.

GLOSSARY

atom—a tiny element that makes up matter

charge—the amount of electricity that is in or on an object; an atom's charge is determined by the balance of electrons and protons within the atom

circuit—a path that goes in a circle, and the beginning and ending are at the same place; electricity travels on a circuit

electron—the part of an atom with a negative charge

neutron—the part of an atom with no charge

nucleus—the center of an atom; a nucleus is made up of neutrons and protons

proton—the part of an atom with a positive charge

transformer—something that changes the voltage of the electricity that goes between power plants and houses; transformers are also used for charging everyday electronics, such as cell phones, electric shavers, and tablets

turbine—an engine powered by water, steam, gas, air, or other fluid; the water, steam, gas, or air moves through the blades of a fanlike device and makes it turn

voltage—the strength of an electrical current; voltage is measured in volts

READ MORE

Carlson Berne, Emma. *Shocking! Electricity*. Energy Everywhere. New York: PowerKids Press, 2013.

Graf, Mike. *How Does a Waterfall Become Electricity?* How Does It Happen? Chicago: Raintree, 2009.

Oxlade, Chris. *Making a Circuit*. It's Electric! Chicago: Heinemann Library, 2012.

MAKE AN ORIGAMI FIREFLY

Glenda simply glows, right? Want to make your own origami firefly? Follow these instructions.

WHAT YOU DO

Folds

Valley folds are shown with a dashed line. One side of the paper is folded against the other like a book. A sharp fold is made by running your finger along the fold line.

Mountain folds are shown with a white dashed and dotted line. The paper should be folded sharply behind the model.

Arrows

single-pointed arrow: Fold the paper in the direction of the arrow.

half-pointed arrow: Fold the paper behind.

1. Start with the colored side down. Valley fold the paper in half.

2. Valley fold to the point on both sides.

3. Valley fold the tip down on both sides.

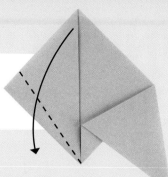

4. Valley fold the top layer. Leave part of the tail showing.

5. Valley fold the top point. Leave part of the white edge showing.

6. Mountain fold both top sides.

7. Valley fold both top sides to create eyes.

INDEX

INTERNET SITES

FactHound offers a safe, fun way to find Internet sites related to this book. All of the sites on FactHound have been researched by our staff.

Here's all you do:

Visit www.facthound.com

Type in this code: 9781479521890

MORE BOOKS in the series:

Diggin' Dirt: Science Adventures with Kitanai the Origami Dog

Wild Weather: Science Adventures with Sonny the Origami Bird

Lookin' for Light: Science Adventures with Manny the Origami Moth

Simply Sound: Science Adventures with Jasper the Origami Bat

Thanks to our advisers for their expertise, research, and advice:
Paul Ohmann, PhD, Associate Professor and Chair of Physics
University of St. Thomas

Terry Flaherty, PhD, Professor of English
Minnesota State University, Mankato

Editor: Shelly Lyons
Designer: Ashlee Suker
Art Director: Nathan Gassman
Production Specialist: Eric Manske
The illustrations in this book were created digitally.

Picture Window Books are published by Capstone,
1710 Roe Crest Drive, North Mankato, Minnesota 56003
www.capstonepub.com

Library of Congress Cataloging-in-Publication Data
Troupe, Thomas Kingsley, author.
Glowing with electricity : science adventures with Glenda
the origami firefly / by Thomas Kingsley Troupe.
pages cm. — (Nonfiction picture books. Origami
science adventures.)
Summary: "Engaging text and colorful illustrations and photos teach
readers about electricity"— Provided by publisher. Audience: 4-8.
Audience: Grade K to 3.
Includes bibliographical references and index.
ISBN 978-1-4795-2189-0 (library binding)
ISBN 978-1-4795-2946-9 (paperback)
ISBN 978-1-4795-3325-1 (ebook PDF)
1. Electricity—Juvenile literature. 2. Fireflies—Juvenile literature.
3. Origami—Juvenile literature. I. Title.
QC527.2.T76 2014
537—dc23   2013034938

Photo credits
Digital illustrations include royalty-free images from Shutterstock.

Capstone Studio: TJ Thoraldson Digital Photography, 22-23;
Shutterstock: Aptyp_koK, 1 (top left), Bryan Busovicki, 11 (bottom),
Igorsky, 13 (bottom), Jan Martin Will, 1 (bottom left), Jim Barber,
cover (left), kosam, 2 (middle right), Stocksnapper, 7 (bottom right),
T.W. van Urk, 13 (top right)

Printed in the United States of America in Stevens Point, Wisconsin.
092013   007768WZS14